AMERICAN HISTORY BY DECADE

The

1970s

Titles in the American History by Decade series include:

The 1900s
The 1910s
The 1920s
The 1930s
The 1940s
The 1950s
The 1960s
The 1970s
The 1980s
The 1990s

AMERICAN HISTORY BY DECADE

The
1970s

Adam Woog

**KIDHAVEN
PRESS**™

THOMSON

™

GALE

San Diego • Detroit • New York • San Francisco • Cleveland
New Haven, Conn. • Waterville, Maine • London • Munich

LIBRARY OF CONGRESS CATALOGING-IN-PUBLICATION DATA

Woog, Adam, 1953–
  The 1970s / by Adam Woog.
    p. cm. — (American History by Decade)
Summary: Discusses the 1970s including the Vietnam War, President Nixon's resignation, the environmental movement, blockbuster movies, and music. Includes bibliographical references (p.) and index.
  ISBN 0-7377-1749-1 (hardback : alk. paper)
  1. United States—History—1969—Juvenile literature. 2. Nineteen seventies—Juvenile literature. [1. United States—History—1969– . 2. Nineteen seventies.]
I. Title. II. Series.
  E855.W58 2004
  973.924—dc22

                                                              2003014868

Printed in the United States of America

Contents

CHAPTER ONE

A Decade of Discontent

For many Americans the seventies were a difficult time. It was a decade of discontent, unease, and disillusion. According to writer David Frum, "Not since the Depression [of the 1930s] had the country been so wracked with woe [misery]. Never—not even during the Depression—had American pride and self-confidence plunged deeper."[1]

Perhaps the biggest cause of this dissatisfaction was the ongoing war in Vietnam. The American military had been in that country since the 1960s. U.S. authorities tried to keep North Vietnam's Communist government from invading South Vietnam.

The situation was very complicated, and the conflict dragged on for many years. It became very difficult for the U.S. forces to leave but also very difficult for them to stay.

For and Against the War

Many Americans were horrified by the war. Thousands of Americans were dying, but the conflict kept dragging on with no end in sight. Americans became bitterly divided over the issue. Some felt that the United States was unfairly interfering in another country's business. Others felt that the U.S. government was doing the right thing.

Throughout the late sixties and into the seventies, large numbers of Americans—most of them young people—took part in antiwar protests. Sometimes these protests turned violent. The worst violence came in 1970, when Ohio National Guardsmen fired on a crowd of young protesters at Kent State University. Four people were killed and nine wounded.

The sight of American troops firing on American citizens shocked the nation. The Kent State tragedy sparked the largest

Protesters demonstrate against the Vietnam War during a rally in Washington, D.C.

round of protests yet, especially on college campuses. Student-led strikes shut down more than five hundred schools nationwide.

The War Ends

President Richard Nixon wanted what he called "peace with honor" in Vietnam. He wanted to end the war but did not

Vietnam and Neighboring Countries Before the Withdrawal of U.S. Troops

American soldiers march through a forest in Vietnam. The war ended in 1975 when U.S. troops left Vietnam.

want to admit defeat. Nixon therefore did things that seemed to contradict each other. He both expanded the U.S. role in the war and worked to end it.

In time, failure to bring an end to the war, as well as mounting pressure by peace activists, forced President Nixon to pull the American military out of Vietnam. In 1975, the last U.S. troops left. After this, the Communist government of North Vietnam invaded the south.

The war's outcome was grim. About 58,000 Americans died, and more than 300,000 were wounded. The conflict cost the United States about $200 billion. More than 184,000 South Vietnamese soldiers died. North Vietnam's casualty figures are not known, but its death toll has been estimated at 900,000. In addition to the military casualties, more than 1 million Vietnamese civilians died.

Antiwar protests had nearly torn America apart. Furthermore, the aftermath of the conflict continued to affect life for virtually every American throughout the seventies and beyond.

Watergate

Although Nixon accomplished several important things during his presidency, many people viewed his leadership as poor. Primarily, Nixon was the center of a scandal that rocked the nation and led to his resignation.

It started with a burglary in a Washington, D.C., office building called the Watergate. In June 1972, five men were caught breaking into the offices of the Democratic National Committee there.

The burglars were working for the committee guiding Nixon's reelection campaign. (Nixon was a Republican.) The burglars wanted to photograph documents belonging to the Democrats and to adjust electronic bugging equipment that had been installed.

Eventually, the five men and two of their associates were convicted of burglary, conspiracy, and wiretapping. Before that could happen, however, Nixon won a landslide victory in the 1972 election.

Bob Woodward and Carl Bernstein, reporters for the *Washington Post*, followed the story further. They uncovered a wide range of scandals, cover-ups, and illegal activities by top Nixon aides.

In 1973, a Senate subcommittee and a special investigator were appointed to look into the matter. Millions of Americans watched the Senate hearings that summer on TV with fascination. Following the growing scandal became a national pastime. Writer/actor Harry Shearer recalls: "Only Super Bowls, wars and the final episodes of beloved sitcoms can bring us together . . . in the way that Watergate television did."[2]

"I Am Not a Crook"

The investigators found proof of many illegal activities. For instance, Nixon had used agencies such as the Internal Revenue Service to harass people on his "enemies list" (a long list of politicians, journalists, entertainers, and academics). Also, the president had tried to force the media to report only news favorable to him.

Furthermore, the Watergate break-in was not a single incident. Nixon's secret unit of operatives, nicknamed "the

Carl Bernstein (left) and Bob Woodward sit in the newsroom of the *Washington Post.*

plumbers," had been employed often to investigate his enemies, using illegal methods such as wiretaps.

Nixon insisted that he did not know anything about the plumbers or any illegal acts. He declared, "I am not a crook."[3]

However, the president had made secret tape recordings of conversations in the White House. When he was forced to hand these over, the recordings proved that he had known about Watergate. Furthermore, they showed that he had tried to cover up the break-in and had tried to bribe the burglars into keeping quiet about his involvement.

Nixon Resigns

Following this startling news, the House of Representatives recommended that Nixon be impeached. **Impeachment** means finding a president guilty of conduct unbecoming to his office. In this case, Nixon was accused of several crimes, including blocking justice.

Demonstrators outside the White House call for President Nixon to be impeached.

Nixon resigned as president in 1974. Here, Nixon flashes the victory sign as he leaves the White House for the last time.

Before he could be impeached, however, Nixon became, in August 1974, the first (and, so far, only) U.S. president to resign. He told the nation, "By taking this action, I hope that I will have hastened the start of that process of healing so desperately needed in America."[4]

Nixon's original vice president, Spiro T. Agnew, had already resigned. (This was over charges of corruption and tax fraud when Agnew was governor of Maryland.) Congressman Gerald R. Ford had taken Agnew's place as vice president. So, when Nixon resigned, Ford became president.

When Ford took the oath of office, he acknowledged that the country was undergoing a difficult time. He declared, "I assume the Presidency under extraordinary circumstances. . . . This is an hour of history that troubles our minds and hurts our hearts."[5]

Pardon

A month later, Ford pardoned Nixon. This meant that the former president could not be tried for any crimes he may have committed. However, many top figures resigned or were fired because of Watergate, and more than thirty were convicted of criminal deeds.

Watergate, along with the agony of Vietnam, had far-reaching results for America. Poll after poll revealed that many citizens no longer trusted their government—a sharp contrast to earlier decades, when people generally had greater faith in politicians.

Furthermore, these events had done much to create a dark mood for the decade. This mood was strengthened by the growing realization that another serious problem loomed over the country: the destruction of the environment.

The Environmental Movement

For many years, only a few people were concerned about things like pollution and population growth. During the 1970s, however, huge numbers of people began to realize that the earth's health was in danger. This awareness created the environmental movement.

Millions of Americans began joining organizations dedicated to helping the planet. Some of these groups, such as the Sierra Club, concentrated on saving wilderness areas. Others, such as Greenpeace, emphasized political action, such as protesting the dumping of radioactive waste. Still others focused on protecting animals that were in danger of **extinction**, such as whales.

A Growing Awareness

A book by naturalist Rachel Carson, *Silent Spring,* was an early warning about the damage that was being done by **pesticides**. Published in 1962, the book set the stage for the birth of the environmental movement.

The start of the movement can be traced to April 22, 1970. This was the first Earth Day. All across the country, an estimated 20 million people took part in various activities.

They cleaned up their neighborhoods, organized rallies, or attended seminars on topics such as recycling and air pollution. Earth Day (which has been observed every year since)

Then and Now

	1970	2000
U.S. population:	204,879,000	281,421,906
Life expectancy:	Female: 74.8 Male: 67.1	Female: 79.5 Male: 74.1
Average yearly salary:	$7,564	$35,305
Unemployment rate:	4.9%	5%

helped ordinary citizens understand that there were many ways to protect their planet's health.

Laws

As a result of people becoming more aware of the environment, many laws to protect it were passed during the decade. In 1970, President Nixon made a public statement supporting this trend. He said, "A major goal for the next ten years for this country must be to restore the cleanliness of the air, the water, the broader problem of population congestion, transport and the like."[6]

That same year, Nixon created the Environmental Protection Agency (EPA). This government agency establishes national standards for environmental quality.

Throughout the decade, Nixon and the presidents who followed him, Gerald Ford and Jimmy Carter, supervised a number of other important changes. For example, Congress passed laws designed to improve the quality of the nation's air and water. Many dangerous pesticides, such as DDT, were banned. Furthermore, laws were passed to protect endangered animals.

People gather in New York's Central Park to meditate during Earth Day of 1971.

The Energy Crisis

One way people could protect the environment was by conserving energy. This was a new concept for most Americans. They were used to using as much energy as they liked, especially from oil (in the form of gasoline and heating oil).

In fact, Americans used a lot of energy. Only 6 percent of the world's population lived in the United States in the early 1970s. Yet, the United States was responsible for 30 percent of the world's energy usage.

More and more, Americans had been relying on supplies of cheap oil from other countries for their energy needs. So it was a huge shock when the flow of foreign oil suddenly decreased.

This ban, called an **embargo**, occurred between October 1973 and March 1974. The Organization of Petroleum Exporting Countries (OPEC), mostly made up of Arab countries, ordered it to protest America's military support of their enemy, Israel.

Signs like this were typical at gas stations around the country during the oil embargo.

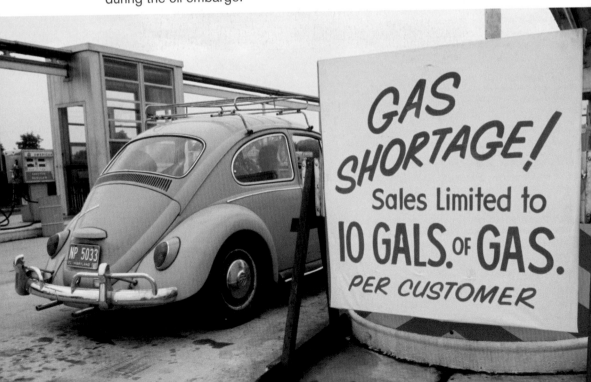

A long line of cars stretches across a bridge as drivers wait for gas. Drivers often waited hours only to learn that the station had run out of gas.

Suddenly, America discovered, there was not enough energy to meet the country's needs. The result was chaos. Writer Pagan Kennedy notes, "The effects of the embargo on Americans' day-to-day life were immediate and crippling."[7]

No Energy

For example, gas stations were forced to close or to limit their sales. All across the country, long lines of cars snaked around the block as hopeful drivers waited for gas. Frequent fights broke out over who was next in line, and near-riots took place when gas stations ran out. When gas could be bought at all, it was expensive: For the first time in U.S. history, it cost over a dollar a gallon.

Nixon had to launch emergency measures. He urged people to lower the thermostats in their houses. To conserve fuel, he also lowered highway speed limits. Furthermore, Nixon urged Americans to use less electricity, and he made daylight saving time effective year-round.

Many businesses and schools shortened their working hours. Whenever possible, people walked or rode bicycles and buses. Many abandoned big, gas-guzzling American cars in favor of smaller, foreign-made cars such as Toyotas. American carmakers responded by making smaller cars, as well.

The Second Energy Crisis

When the embargo ended, oil prices dropped. However, a second energy crisis occurred in 1979 when Iran, an OPEC country that was experiencing political turmoil, stopped all exports. The other OPEC nations then raised their prices.

President Jimmy Carter started many programs to create or conserve energy in the wake of this shortage. For example, his administration sponsored experiments with alternative sources of energy, such as wind and solar power. Also, serious experimental development of electric cars began during this period.

People could get grants, loans, and tax credits for installing energy-saving devices, such as insulation, in their homes. Programs to recycle materials such as metal were started. Also, laws were passed making home appliances, such as clothes dryers, more energy efficient.

Carter made personal appeals as well. For example, he appeared on television in a warm sweater, asking citizens to lower their thermostats. He even installed solar panels on the White House roof and a wood stove in its living quarters. (These were later removed.) Carter stated about the need to conserve energy, "With the exception of preventing war, this is the greatest challenge that our country will face in our lifetimes."[8]

Nuclear Power

One source of energy, nuclear power, seemed especially promising. President Nixon had been very interested in promoting it. He had authorized the building of many nuclear facilities.

A man rides a bike carrying bags of aluminum cans. Recycling programs were implemented across the country during the energy crisis.

However, many people were concerned about the safety of nuclear power. These concerns were intensified in 1979, after the worst accident in U.S. nuclear history—when the Three Mile Island facility in Harrisburg, Pennsylvania, nearly melted down.

A woman and her daughter walk near the Three Mile Island nuclear plant in Harrisburg.

There were no immediate deaths or injuries from this accident. However, about fifty thousand people had to temporarily leave town, the town's schools shut down, and many businesses closed. Also, several hundred local people experienced strange illnesses afterwards, including vomiting, hair loss, and skin rashes. Furthermore, exposure to radiation may have caused cancer in some residents.

After Three Mile Island, the government made changes in the way nuclear power plants were regulated. Also, there was a serious slowdown in the growth of the nuclear-reactor industry. This once-promising source of energy proved to be bitterly disappointing.

Environmental problems were just some of the problems of the seventies. When times are tough, people often look for ways to escape. Writer Pagan Kennedy notes, "[M]any people would rather remember what was on TV in the seventies than what was actually going on in their lives."[9] One pastime that helped people forget their troubles was going to the movies.

CHAPTER THREE

Blockbuster Movies

S ome of the best movies of the seventies, such as *China-town* and *The Godfather,* were serious dramas. However, the big news in Hollywood during the decade was the spectacular success of blockbuster movies—action-packed adventure/fantasy films with lots of dazzling special effects. Blockbuster movies dominated Hollywood in the last half of the 1970s. To a large degree, they still do.

The stories of two young directors, Steven Spielberg and George Lucas, were closely tied to this trend. Together and separately, Spielberg and Lucas virtually created the modern blockbuster. In the process, they became two of the most influential men in Hollywood—and changed American movie history.

Jaws

Spielberg was only twenty-seven when his first major film was released in 1975. It was called *Jaws,* a suspense movie about a terrifying killer shark.

The movie did not at first seem like anything special, and no one expected it to be a hit. For one thing, the director was unknown, and it had no big stars.

Also, the movie's production had many problems. The crew found it difficult to control the three twenty-five-foot mechanical sharks that were used. Also, it was almost impossible to film scenes on open water.

Many days were wasted on repairs and problems. This delayed shooting. The cost of making *Jaws* rose far above its original budget. The studio that was financing the movie nearly closed the production down before it was finished.

To everyone's surprise, *Jaws* was an instant hit. Audiences loved the movie for its suspense and scariness. It soon became the most successful film in history up to that time. The movie made millions of dollars; it also turned Spielberg and actor Richard Dreyfuss into international stars.

Actor Richard Dreyfuss stands next to a mechanical great white shark on the set of *Jaws*.

Jaws cemented Spielberg's reputation. As his many fans know, almost all of the projects that Spielberg did after it have also been huge hits. In the seventies, the most notable of these was *Close Encounters of the Third Kind*—a blockbuster film about a group of people who are mysteriously affected by UFO sightings.

Star Wars

In 1997, two years after *Jaws* was released, Spielberg's friend George Lucas released a science-fiction movie called *Star Wars*. Along with *Jaws*, *Star Wars* truly launched the seventies blockbuster era.

Star Wars premiered in 1977. It became a big moneymaker and made actor Harrison Ford (right) into an international star.

Like *Jaws*, *Star Wars* at first seemed to have little chance of success. For one thing, science-fiction fantasies were not in fashion. They had never made much money; besides, their poor special effects generally looked terrible. Also, the making of *Star Wars*, like that of *Jaws*, had been chaotic. It was shot on a tiny budget, and many things went wrong.

The movie also had no big stars in it, and there was almost no advance publicity before it opened. Not even the director thought it would be a hit. He recalled, "I thought it was too wacky for the general public. I just [figured that] I'm going to do this kind of crazy thing, and it'll be fun, and that will be that." [10]

He was wrong. *Star Wars* opened in only thirty-two theaters around the country, but the theater owners were astonished to find long lines forming hours early on opening night. Word had already spread about the movie.

Star Wars was an immediate hit. It quickly smashed all previous box-office records. Within six months it passed *Jaws* to become the biggest moneymaker in history. Like *Jaws*, *Star Wars* also made its unknown director, George Lucas, and leading actor, Harrison Ford, into international superstars.

"Oh, Another First!"

The amazing success of *Star Wars* and *Jaws* caught Hollywood by surprise. Movie studios frantically began trying to repeat the achievements of these movies. Dozens of potential blockbusters—some of them good, many of them bad—were produced in the following years. They mostly used the same basic formula: fast action, an element of fantasy, and eye-popping visual effects.

The rise of blockbusters had a major impact on the field of special effects. Before *Star Wars* and *Jaws*, this was only a minor part of filmmaking. Generally, only one or two small effects were needed in a movie, if at all.

The special effects of *Star Wars* contributed to the film's success. Many films attempted to duplicate the blockbuster by using dazzling special effects.

In the seventies that changed. Dozens of companies quickly formed just to create special effects. One example was Industrial Light & Magic, which was created by George Lucas during the making of *Star Wars* (and today is the movie industry's dominant effects company).

The focus on special effects not only expanded the field; it also radically changed what special-effects artists were capable of creating. Before *Star Wars* and *Jaws,* most special effects looked cheap and corny. During the seventies, however, techniques dramatically improved.

Since it was almost a brand-new art, special-effects artists had to constantly invent new ways to achieve their goals. Effects artist Richard Edlund, who worked on *Star Wars*, recalls that so many new techniques were invented on the set of that movie that it became almost routine: "Some guy across the stage would say, 'Oh, another first!' Some other new thing had been done that we knew hadn't been done before." [11]

Special Effects Rule

As a result, the field of special visual effects is today well established. It routinely uses computer-generated graphics, miniature models, makeup, and other advanced techniques. These methods are used to create elaborate, detailed worlds that otherwise would exist only in the imaginations of the moviemakers.

Special effects, like the computer-generated dinosaurs of *Jurassic Park,* are responsible for the success of many of today's blockbusters.

Throughout the rest of the twentieth century and into the present one, special effects—and blockbuster movies—have continued to dominate Hollywood. As millions of moviegoers know, Spielberg and Lucas followed up their 1970s successes with more triumphs, including the Indiana Jones movies (which they made together).

The two also inspired many other directors to create their own visions in the form of blockbuster movies. Among the notable special-effects blockbusters of the seventies and eighties were *Alien, Ghostbusters, Gremlins, Blade Runner, Who Framed Roger Rabbit, An American Werewolf in London, Poltergeist,* the first *Star Trek* movies, Spielberg's *E.T. the Extra-Terrestrial,* and Lucas's *Star Wars* sequels. Each one sought to top previous movies with the power of its amazing visual effects.

Of course, movies were not the only entertainment in the 1970s. People also eagerly listened and danced to the latest music.

CHAPTER FOUR

Punk and Disco

Punk and disco were two of the most important pop-culture events of the 1970s. Both movements had a strong impact on the decade's music and clothes.

Rebellion

Punk started as a rebellion against the smooth pop-rock that was often heard in the early seventies. Punk rockers wanted to re-create rock's original feeling instead. Back in the 1950s, many of the first rock-and-roll songs had been rough, short, impolite, and loud. The punk revolution of 1975–1976, inspired by this spirit, tried to break rock into pieces, according to journalist Al Spicer: "Now and again, [bands come along] and take a sledgehammer to the definition of rock music."[12]

Punk did this by stripping rock to its basics: blasting guitar, bass, and drums; frantic rhythms; and screaming vocals. Punk fashion was equally striking: wild clothes (such as decorated black leather jackets), bizarre accessories (such as cheeks pierced with diaper pins), and extreme haircuts (such as multicolored Mohawks).

Punk shows were just as outrageous. The musicians could often barely play. Audiences and musicians were aggressive, often throwing beer cans and spitting at each other. The dance floor was a mass of bodies bashing into one another. Fights were common, onstage and off.

Punk rockers wore extreme hairstyles, makeup, and jewelry.

Punk's Origins

Punk developed as an underground, almost secret, movement in two cities: London and New York. American punk developed just before the English version.

New York's punk scene emerged around 1974, mainly in two nightclubs: Max's Kansas City and CBGB. Among the bands that appeared regularly there were Television, Talking Heads, Blondie, the New York Dolls, and the Patti Smith Group.

Each of these bands had a distinctive style. For instance, the Dolls liked tough songs and glittery costumes, and Patti Smith was a mystical but hard-rocking singer-poet.

Perhaps the most influential of these bands was the Ramones. The Ramones had an almost cartoonlike image. Band members always wore torn jeans, old sneakers, ripped T-shirts, and leather jackets. Ramones songs were ultrafast and ultraloud, with intentionally silly lyrics, and the band's unofficial slogan was "Gabba Gabba Hey!"

Joey Ramone, lead singer of the punk group the Ramones, performs onstage.

London Punk

The Ramones was the first punk band to tour widely. As a result, it influenced musicians elsewhere in the United States. The band also played a show in London in 1976 that inspired many musicians in the growing punk movement there. Critic Kurt Loder writes, "The Ramones . . . landed in this flabbed-out scene like a boulder on a box of sugar-cream doughnuts."[13]

Inspired by the dynamic Ramones show, London punk bands like the Clash and the Slits, which were just getting started, became very popular. British punk was generally angrier and more political than its American partner. England

The London punk band the Clash (pictured) was inspired by the Ramones.

The Sex Pistols, with lead singer Johnny Rotten (pictured), was the top punk band in London.

had serious unemployment, a depressed economy, and frequent racial violence. The lyrics of songs such as "No Future" reflected the anger and frustration many musicians felt.

The top London punk band was the Sex Pistols. Its front man was Johnny Rotten. Rotten could barely sing, but he had a powerful presence. He was also good at creating controversy with his outspoken opinions, spiked and multicolored hair, heavy boots, and pinned-together clothing.

Punk Spreads and Fades

Punk spread quickly, inspired by the New York and London bands. In the United States, strong punk scenes formed in such cities as Los Angeles, Cleveland, Seattle, and San Francisco.

The punk movement faded away by the end of the decade, as newer styles took over. However, punk left behind important legacies. Musically, it has directly influenced virtually every style of rock since.

Also, punk's emphasis on democracy and equality remained. Punks believed that anyone could get up onstage and play; it was not necessary to have much musical talent. And if anyone could be in a band, then anyone could produce a record, start a fan magazine, or promote a concert. This attitude has strongly influenced today's independent recording scene, which has developed separately from the major record labels.

The Beginnings of Disco

Unlike punk rockers, some people in the seventies did not care much about making political statements. They just wanted to dance. Disco was music made just for dancing, and it was just for them.

In the 1960s there had been a fad for clubs called **discotheques**, where people danced to records instead of live bands. New York's gay and black communities adopted this in the early 1970s and created their own style of music.

Disco, as this music came to be called, emphasized a steady, nonstop rhythm. It was mostly instrumental; the lyrics (when there were any) usually just urged people to dance more. There were many different styles, from mechanical "Eurodisco" to the lush, symphonic "Philly Sound"—but disco always had a thumping rhythm.

Disco remained underground until the release in 1977 of the movie *Saturday Night Fever.* Featuring a star-making performance by John Travolta and songs by several groups, notably the Bee Gees, the movie brought disco to a wide audience.

Disco Explodes

Saturday Night Fever was a huge hit, and its sound track sold millions. Suddenly, disco was everywhere. Everyone wanted

Actor John Travolta dances in a scene from *Saturday Night Fever.* The movie made disco popular across the country.

to dress like the movie's stars and dance to disco's rhythm. Many different kinds of people found they liked the music, writes critic Tom Smucker: "The audience . . . cut across barriers of age, class, sex, race, and nationality."[14]

Disco clothes were part of the attraction. Outrageous dresses and hot pants for women, polyester shirts and gold medallions for men, plus uncomfortable and impractical platform shoes for everyone. (Thanks to these faddish clothes, the seventies has often been called "the decade that style forgot.")

A woman shops for platform shoes. The shoes were extremely popular in the 1970s.

A teenager wears a typical 1970s outfit of hot pants, knee socks, and platform shoes.

As disco's popularity soared, dozens of musicians not normally associated with the style tried to sing it. The Rolling Stones, Frank Sinatra, and Broadway star Ethel Merman were just a few of the many famous nondisco musicians who made disco records.

By 1978, 40 percent of all singles and albums on the Billboard Hot 100 (a record-industry chart) were disco oriented. By 1979, about two thousand radio stations had all-disco formats, and there were about twenty thousand discos across the country.

Disco Fades Away

Disco proved to be an intense but short fad. By 1980, it was dead. Like punk, it was succeeded by other, newer forms of music.

However, disco left a strong legacy. It has strongly influenced the dance music of later decades. Many recent styles—including house, techno, industrial, trance, and rap—are direct descendants of disco. The influence of disco, as well as punk and other seventies phenomena, will no doubt continue well into the future.

Notes

Chapter One: A Decade of Discontent

1. David Frum, *How We Were: The 70s, the Decade That Brought You Modern Life—For Better or Worse.* New York: Perseus, 2000, p. 289.
2. Harry Shearer, "The Quitter," in *Rolling Stone: The Seventies.* Boston: Little, Brown, 1998, p. 108.
3. Quoted in Frum, *How We Were*, p. 26.
4. Quoted in *America's Century.* New York: Dorling Kindersley, 2000, p. 324.
5. Quoted in "Gerald R. Ford," White House website. www.whitehouse.gov.

Chapter Two: The Environmental Movement

6. Quoted in Victor Bondi, ed., *American Decades: 1970–1979.* Detroit: Gale Research, 1995, p. 477.
7. Pagan Kennedy, *Platforms: A Microwaved Cultural Chronicle of the 1970s.* New York: St. Martin's Press, 1994, p. 40.
8. Quoted in *America's Century*, p. 334.
9. Kennedy, *Platforms*, p. 5.

Chapter Three: Blockbuster Movies

10. Quoted in "The Force Is Back," *Time*, February 10, 1997, p. 68.
11. Quoted in Dale Pollock, *Skywalking: The Life and Times of George Lucas.* New York: Harmony, 1983, p. 176.

Chapter Four: Punk and Disco

12. Al Spicer, "The Sex Pistols," in Jonathan Buckley and Mark Ellingham, eds., *Rock: The Rough Guide.* London: Rough Guides, 1996, p. 769.

13. Kurt Loder, *Bat Chain Puller.* New York: St. Martin's Press, 1990, p. 367.
14. Tom Smucker, "Disco," in Jim Miller, ed., *The Rolling Stone Illustrated History of Rock & Roll.* New York: Random House, 1980, p. 427.

Glossary

discotheques: Nightclubs of the sixties where people danced to records instead of live bands.

embargo: A ban on bringing certain products into a country.

extinction: No longer in existence.

impeachment: A process by which the U.S. Congress finds a president guilty of conduct unbecoming to the office.

pesticides: Chemicals used to destroy harmful insects and other pests.

For Further Exploration

Robert Gartner, *Working Together Against the Destruction of the Environment.* New York: Rosen, 1994. One of many good books for young readers about the environmental movement.

Sarah Gilmour, *The 70s: Punks, Glam Rockers, & New Romantics.* Milwaukee: Gareth Stevens, 1999. Part of the 20th Century Fashion series, this is a well-illustrated introduction to some of the outrageous clothing fashions of the decade.

Adam Woog, *Steven Spielberg.* San Diego, CA: KidHaven Press, 2003. This brief biography is part of the Inventors and Creators series.

David K. Wright, *War in Vietnam.* Chicago: Childrens Press, 1989. A four-volume series thoroughly covering the conflict in Southeast Asia.

Index

Picture Credits

About the Author

Adam Woog is the author of over forty books for adults, young adults, and children. He lives with his wife and daughter in Seattle, Washington.